HUMAN RESOURCES GUIDE TO SOCIAL MEDIA RISKS

HUMAN RESOURCES GUIDE TO SOCIAL MEDIA RISKS

JESSE TORRES

To Anne

CONTENTS

INTRODUCTION 1

SOCIAL MEDIA PRIMER.. 3

   Types of Social Media 4

   Social Media for Personal Use 8

   Social Media for Business Use..9

   Conclusion 10

SOCIAL MEDIA IN THE WORKPLACE 11

   Recruitment Through Social Media 12

   Employee Use of Social Media...16

      Social Media Challenges..18

      Organizational Versus Personal Social Media Usage....20

      Employees as Brand Ambassadors...............................22

      Let Employees Respond in their Own Voice..................26

      Honest and Transparent Communications 27

      Employee Disclaimers...30

      Protecting Intellectual Property Rights..........................31

      Expectation of Privacy...32

      Employee Training 35

   Social Media-Based Terminations.......................................37

   Action Items 41

CONCLUSION 45

ABOUT THE AUTHOR 47

BIBLIOGRAPHY 49

HUMAN RESOURCES GUIDE TO SOCIAL MEDIA RISKS

INTRODUCTION

According to Marc Gobé in his book "*emotional branding,*" (Allworth Press, 2009), "the Web has fast-tracked careers, turned unknowns into celebrities, built and destroyed brands and reputations, and – against all odds – helped elect a black candidate President of the United States." This phenomenon has occurred as a result of achieving a tipping point in social media usage. While the exact date that social media became ubiquitous in American life is unknown, rest assured that we have without a doubt entered the Golden Age of Social Media.

Global consulting firm Deloitte LLP (Deloitte.com) conducted a social media workplace risk assessment as part of its *2009 Ethics &Workplace Survey*. The Survey found that 58% of executives surveyed agreed that social media should be a board room issue. However, only 15% admitted that it is actually discussed at the board level. The survey also found that only 22% of companies have formal policies in place that dictate how employees can use social media, and only 17% have implemented a program dedicated to monitoring and mitigating risks related to social media.

This Guide is about social media risks and the employment lifecycle. While plenty of guidance exists relative to social media marketing, strategic planning, business development and other related topics, very little has been done to address social media-related risks and human resources. As this Guide will demonstrate, social media risks relative to human resources activities are growing. This Guide will assist human resources professionals in identifying and mitigating social media-related risks before they manifest into damaging events that can take a toll on an organization's reputation and profitability.

A common historical response to social media has been to deny its existence within the organizational walls. As this Guide will show, it is no longer possible for organizations to bury their heads in the sand and ignore social media's presence. Social media is not only here, it's there, and there, and everywhere. Organizations no longer have the luxury of escaping social media's influence in the workplace. In fact, the risks posed by social media are greatest within organizations that fail to acknowledge its existence.

The goal of this Guide is to make the case that all organizations, regardless of their involvement in social media activities, are subject to social media risks in the workplace. As such, a desired outcome of this Guide is to assist organizations in implementing social media guidance related to human resources management. This guidance, in the form of policies and procedures, will protect organizations against the risks posed by social media, and in some cases, will provide organizations with the confidence to accept social media as a strategic objective.

SOCIAL MEDIA PRIMER

For those unfamiliar with social media, this chapter briefly discusses the social media phenomenon at the 50,000-foot level.

Social media was born from the combination of the Internet and social marketing efforts that resulted in a form of marketing that utilizes Internet-based tools (the "media" part) for sharing and discussing information (the "social" part). Social media turns Internet users into creators of user-generated content through the use of comments, videos, blogs, wikis, photos, online reviews, location-based information and other content.

For example, Facebook, the current grand daddy of social media platforms, permits users to generate a wide array of content. It is the ability of ordinary Internet users (peers) to create and consume content that has made social media the

Internet's rock star. According to Sorav Jain, in a November 2010 Social Media Today blog post, 78% of consumers trust peer recommendations on social media sites versus only 14% of consumers trusting mass media advertising. Consistent with this data, Mashable.com's Adam Ostrow stated in a March 2009 blog post that "by the end of 2008, social networking had overtaken email in terms of worldwide reach." As such, it has become clear that social media's popularity and value has resulted due to the democratization of information on the Internet. The ability to comment, opine and share on social media sites has fueled social media's growth to the extent that its use has transformed not only the personal habits of users, but the workplaces in which these individuals operate.

Types of Social Media

There are many types of social media sites. Blogger Linda Fulkerson does a great job of classifying social media sites on her blog, *On Blogging Well* (www.OnBloggingWell.com), into 23 different varieties.

- **Blogs:** These sites include personal and corporate online journals. Many corporate blogs are maintained by the organization such as Microsoft's *IEBlog* (http://blogs.msdn.com/b/ie/) or Vons *Today at Vons* blog (http://community.vons.com/t5/Our-Blog/bg-p/swy001). Other corporate blogs are maintained by public blogging platforms such as WordPress.com, TypePad.com, and Blogger.com.

- **Social Networking Sites:** These sites focus on building relationships among people. Common social networking sites include Facebook.com and MySpace.com.

- **Social News Sites:** These sites accept and distribute news stories by users. One of the most popular social news sites is Digg.com.

- **Social Measuring Sites:** These sites measure the quality of content that exists on the Internet. A popular social measuring site is Technorati.com.

- **Microblogging Sites:** These sites deliver content in short bursts. The most popular microblogging site is Twitter.com, which delivers information in bursts of no more than 140 characters.

- **Social Bookmarking Sites:** These sites allow users to share, organize, and search bookmarks of web resources. A popular social bookmarking site is delicious.com (formerly del.icio.us).

- **Social Q&A Sites:** These sites allow users to submit questions or answer questions. Two popular social Q & A sites include Answers.com and Yahoo! Answers (anwers.yahoo.com).

- **Video Sharing Sites:** These sites allow users to upload and comment on videos. The most popular video sharing site is YouTube.com.

- **Photo Sharing Sites:** These sites allow users to upload and comment on photos. Popular photo sharing sites include Flickr.com and Twitpic.com.

- **Social Search Sites:** These sites are social media-enabled search sites where users can create communities. The most popular search sites are Yahoo.com and Google.com.

- **Professional Network Sites:** These sites are a combination virtual business card holders and social networks. These sites enable users to recommend connections, share information about industry-related events, post resumes, and other features that relate to professional matters. The most popular professional network site is LinkedIn.com.

- **Niche Communities:** These sites have evolved from message boards into full-fledged communities. Niche communities are focused on serving individuals with specific needs, such at Match.com for singles and Classmates.com for school alumni.

- **Social Email:** Social email platforms include Google Buzz.

- **Comment Communities:** Popular comment community Disqus.com describes itself as a platform that helps users build an active community from a web site's audience.

- **Regional Social Media Sites:** These sites are geographically focused. An example is Examiner.com.

- **Podcasting Communities:** These sites are social networks that connect podcasters, advertisers, and listeners. An example is Blubrry.com.

- **Blog Networks:** These sites are similar to niche communities. These sites are comprised of blogs that address specific topics such as technology, politics, etc. Popular blog networks include Gawker.com, Jezebel.com, and Gizmodo.com.

- **Blogging Communities:** Blogging communities encourage bloggers to share and interact with one another as well as create regular blog posts. Popular blogging communities include BlogHer.com and LiveJournal.com.

- **Presentation-Sharing Sites:** These sites allow users to share their presentations. The most popular presentation sharing site is SlideShare.com.

- **Content-Driven Communities:** These sites, referred to as "wikis," provide and collect encyclopedia type information. The most common wiki is Wikipedia.org.

- **Product-Based Communities:** These sites are tied to electronic commerce sites where goods are bought and sold. These communities allow the exchange of information related to the products and services that are being bought and sold. These communities are known for providing ratings and reviews as well as provide question and answer forums. The most popular product-based communities are Ebay.com and Amazon.com.

- **Review & Recommendation Sites:** These sites have features similar to those on product-based communities. However, these sites are not necessarily associated with products or services. For example, TripAdvisor.com relates to travel and Shelfari.com relates to books.

- **Social Media Sites that Defy Definition:** This category relates to sites that cannot be easily classified.

Social Media for Personal Use

Studies have found that social media significantly affects the manner in which people communicate with each other. Social media affects how users make decisions, socialize, learn, entertain themselves, and do their shopping. Research has led to the conclusion that social media has caused a shift in the influence of consumers at the expense of mass media such as television, radio, and newspapers. This democratization process has significantly reduced the effectiveness of mass marketing campaigns and has given the consumer more choice in selecting which messages to listen to and which messages to create.

In June 2010, Performics (www.Performics.com) released a report, "S-Net (*The Impact of Social Media*)," based on a study that explored how social media affects consumers' lives and affects communication, shopping and other activities. According to Performics, the findings concluded that social media definitely affects the online behavior of consumers. Performics CEO Daina Middleton stated that "social networking has greatly contributed to the shift from strict consumerism to more lively, two-way participation between brands and everyday customers. It's a groundswell of technology – enabled word of mouth, and many of the brands involved in these active discussions are effectively satisfying their fans."

Rather than merely consume the messages, through social media the consumer is now becoming both consumer and creator of messages. For example, a consumer may decide to buy this Guide based on positive book reviews posted on Amazon.com. Upon reading this book, the same consumer may post his own positive review, further encouraging more consumers to purchase this Guide. This series of user-generated reviews is increasingly becoming more valuable than the most sophisticated marketing messages produced by professionals. The vast and exponentially growing knowledge base created by comments, product reviews, and other publicly shared information provides consumers with valued feedback that allows more informed decisions.

The shift from professionals to peers is forcing businesses to deal in a more honest and transparent manner or risk losing the business to a competitor that does. While social media presents challenges to businesses, it also provides opportunities to organizations that embrace the change and work within the new paradigm. The message that is penetrating the business community is that businesses that ignore social media do so at the risk of becoming irrelevant.

Social Media for Business Use

The rapid growth of social media as an influential communications channel caught many businesses unprepared. While many companies promptly jumped into social media and accepted the challenges, the majority of businesses initially decided to sit on the sidelines due to reasons such as dismissing social media as a fad, lack of technical understanding, or fear of the unknown.

Nora Ganim Barnes and Eric Mattson, researchers at the University of Massachusetts Dartmouth Center for Marketing Research (http://www1.umassd.edu), conducted a study (*"Social Media in the Inc. 500: The First Longitudinal Study"*) of corporate adoption of social media between 2007 and 2008 by the Inc. 500, a list of the fastest-growing private U.S. companies compiled annually by Inc. Magazine. The study concluded that social media had penetrated parts of the business world at a tremendous speed. The report also indicated that corporate familiarity with and usage of social media within the Inc. 500 had nearly doubled from 2007 to 2008. Similar results were reported by the University of Maryland's Smith School of Business (www.rhsmith.umd.edu) (*"Social Media Adoption By U.S. Small Businesses Doubles Since 2009"*) as part of a December 2009 survey of small businesses.

Social media well deployed within an organization can provide several benefits:

1. It can cultivate a community of informed and supportive customers and other stakeholders (shareholders, vendors, etc.);

2. It can enhance the organization's brand;

3. It can assist the organization in strengthening relationships with customers and other stakeholders; and,

4. It can turn customers into evangelists/promoters of the organization.

As a result of social media, the user, not the organization, has become the most important influencer. According to Yahoo! Northern Europe's Glen Drury, "whereas marketing with traditional media like newspapers, television and news websites was about delivering a message; marketing with social media is about building a relationship and conversation with your audience. Marketing is no longer one dimensional; it is now a two-way process engaging a brand and an audience. Marketing within social media is not just about telling and giving a message, rather it is about receiving and exchanging perceptions and ideas."

Conclusion

As stated by Brian Solis (www.BrianSolis.com) in *The Essential Guide to Social Media*, social media is much more than user-generated content. It is a mix of technologies that together empower consumers by providing them with a continuous and flexible flow of democratized information that is not tainted by commercial influences. It is driven by people in the communities where they communicate and congregate.

SOCIAL MEDIA IN THE WORKPLACE

As more and more organizations see the value in deploying a social media strategy and as social media platforms continue to attract new users from every conceivable demographic, the lines between personal and professional social media use are becoming increasingly blurred. According to eMarketer's (www.emarketer.com) December 2010 report, *"Social Media in the Marketing Mix: Budgeting for 2011,"* in 2011, "four out of five US businesses with 100 or more employees will use social media marketing. That's a dramatic change from 2008 when just 42% of companies marketed via social media. As consumer usage of social media continues to increase in the US and around the world, marketers have transitioned from cautious engagement to full deployment."

The increased use of social media in the workplace has begun to create very significant benefits for organizations. Unfortunately, these benefits have been joined by equally significant challenges. This chapter will describe the role that social media can play in the employment lifecycle. Organizations can utilize social media to supplement candidate application information to create a very complete candidate assessment. Social media can also turn every employee into an organizational evangelist, helping the organization penetrate the market like never before. Conversely, through the viral capabilities of social media, a disgruntled army of one employee can turn itself into a potential army of millions, unleashing significant damage to the organization's brand, and in many cases, with little recourse to the organization.

This chapter provides guidance relative to use of social media as a recruiting tool. The chapter also addresses the challenges posed by employee social media usage. The chapter speaks to the need to treat every employee as a "Brand Ambassador" for the purpose of ensuring that all employees are aware of their power as promoters of the organization. Related to "Brand Ambassadors" is the topic of employee training and the processes each organization should establish to protect itself from employee-based social media risks. Also addressed in this chapter is the issue of employee privacy and whether employees can reasonably maintain an expectation of privacy when utilizing social media in the workplace. The chapter concludes with guidance relative to employee terminations related to acts conducted on social media platforms. The chapter addresses both current case law as well as statutory requirements that come into play when disciplining an employee for deeds related to social media.

The objective of this chapter is to provide organizations with a survey of the risks that exist relative to social media in the workplace. Knowledge of such risks will enable each organization to craft a formal, written social media policy that is consistent with its mission, goals, and appetite for risk.

Recruitment Through Social Media

The traditional view among human resources professionals is that extraneous information should not be considered as part of the recruiting process. The fear is that the use of such information may run afoul of human resource laws, creating potential legal risks. However, given the rich and deep reservoir of information accessible through social media, many organizations are currently using or are considering use of social media as a source of information when evaluating potential candidates.

Social media's value, when it comes to employee recruitment, is its ability to access applicant information that is generally not available through the traditional interview process. Through social media, organizations are able to learn much more about applicants than can be gleaned from a one-page resume. Social media can provide detailed information regarding an applicant's professional background, experience, skills, competencies, and other qualitative factors that may help during the candidate evaluation process. As such, it is no surprise that human resources departments and recruiters are considering how to mine social media for nuggets of information that will ensure hiring decisions are sound and will result in the hiring of strong, productive team members. However, as noted below, access to this information comes at a cost.

To the extent that organizations choose to utilize social media for recruiting purposes, employees responsible for collecting social media-based employment information must be trained to stay focused on capturing and evaluating only the information that addresses the applicant's qualifications and expertise. Capturing and evaluating unrelated information may lead to false impressions of applicants as well as potentially unlawful actions.

Prior to the existence of social media, candidates were easily able to maintain segregated personal and professional lives. However, as social media has become ubiquitous, it is much more difficult for candidates to effectively separate their personal lives from their professional lives. As more and more people participate on social media platforms and become increasingly transparent regarding the events in their personal and professional lives through updates, photos and other information, personal and professional activities have become woven into a single fabric. As such, the challenge with using social media to conduct background checks on applicants is that it is difficult, if not impossible, to determine where the personal activity ends and professional activity begins.

No two candidates are identical. Every candidate is unique with a distinct personality, experience, education, background, etc. To the extent that organizations access social media information, they must be aware of the fact that everyone is different. Hiring managers may opine that a particular candidate possesses "quirky" or unusual characteristics. For example, a hiring manager may find photos of the candidate dressed as a superhero while attending a comic book convention. There is nothing wrong with candidates that possess such "unique" qualities. Human resources personnel and others involved in the candidate evaluation process should stay focused on determining whether the candidate's professional qualifications meet the requirements of the position. An adverse hiring decision based upon the "unusual" information may result in passing up on an otherwise strong candidate. In addition, such actions may violate "legal activities" laws that prohibit employers from taking certain actions on the basis of "personal time" activities.

At times organizations using social media as part of the recruitment process may come across other information that suggests that the candidate is not suitable for the position. Such information may relate to illegal drug use, evidence of a poor work ethic, inadequate writing/communication skills, abusive attitude towards prior employers, racist or other discriminating tendencies, or general poor judgment as evidenced by the content of the applicant's social media pages. To the extent that the organization finds such information, it may be justified in declining the applicant. In such a case, the decision should be well documented as the applicant may request access to such information based upon rights conferred by the federal Fair Credit Reporting Act and similar state statutes. An option for the organization when faced with such derogatory information is to confirm the accuracy of such information with the applicant. This, however, should not be done without legal advice as it may result in additional challenges to the extent that the applicant is denied employment.

Organizations that utilize social media as part of the recruitment process should include within the application package, a written notice that the background check may involve a review of any "publicly-available" information, including social media sites. Once the disclosure is provided it is important to keep any inquiry limited to information that is publicly available. In other words, the organization should not require that applicants provide passwords to their social media accounts nor should it require that applicants "friend," "like" or otherwise grant the organization access to information that would not otherwise be publicly accessible. Such demands, besides being extraordinarily invasive, may violate federal and state privacy statutes. Also, the information collected and subsequently considered, should not include any prohibited information such as race, age, disability, religion, sexual orientation, etc.

The February 2010 issue of *Practical Law: The Journal* (PracticalLaw.com) lists several major risks associated with social media usage as part of the recruiting process:

- Discrimination violations due to adverse employment decisions based on protected class information learned through social media;

- National Labor Relations Act violations due to employment actions inconsistent with the National Labor Relations Act; and,

- Violations of the Fair Credit Reporting Act and its state equivalents as a result of the use of consumer reports in conducting background checks without providing the required adverse action disclosure.

Based upon the potential legal challenges, it is essential that an organization first determine whether the benefits of using social media in the recruitment process outweigh the risks. To the extent that the organization decides to utilize social media as part of the recruiting process, it must develop a policy that addresses the applicable risks. Human resources personnel and other employees involved in the candidate screening process should be well trained to understand the risks associated with using social media. The organization should include within its social media or human resources policy, guidance relative to the applicable laws such as the National Labor Relations Act, Fair Credit Reporting Act, etc. The policy should also address the information gathering process, including the documentation and consideration of only permissible information. This section of the policy will not only provide essential guidance, it can also assist in the event the organization is sued by an applicant alleging consideration of prohibited information obtained through from social media platforms.

Employee Use of Social Media

One of the most commonly discussed issues regarding social media and business is whether employees should be permitted to access social media platforms during the work day. The Internet is full of debate for and against employee use of social media. Critics state that employee use of social media at work will result in a waste of the organization's valuable resources as well as potentially endanger the organization. Detractors state that employee use of social media can harm the organization as a result of thoughtless social media interactions that disclose trade secrets and other confidential information. These opponents state that employees may also create legal liability as a result of the potential for disparaging, harassing, and other comments that give rise to legal action by fellow employees and third parties.

Proponents of social media acknowledge that risks exist but that the potential benefits outweigh the risks so long as the risks are well managed. Supporters of employee use of social media point to social media's ability to significantly increase brand awareness in an effective and economical manner. Also touted is the potential that social media has for increasing sales as a result of an effective social media marketing initiative that includes employees as "Brand Ambassadors." Other benefits include increased goodwill for organizations that act in an honest and transparent manner as well as the benefit to the organization for developing a communal environment that listens to the outside world.

Employee use of social media is not right for all organizations. While some organizations may find it beneficial relative to business development, branding, and customer service, other organizations may determine that the workforce has no business use for social media. Whether or not an organization embarks on a strategy that permits employee use of social media is dependent upon the organization's mission, goals, and appetite for risk. To the extent that an organization permits some form of employee use of social media in the workplace, it must ensure that employee social media usage is managed properly.

While banning social media access at work may reduce some risks, it does not completely eliminate them. For example, with Internet-enabled phones and other devices, employees may continue to access social media platforms during the work day, creating the loss of employee productivity. Also, comments made on social media platforms that create exposure for organizations or that disclose confidential information, may occur during an employee's personal time.

In August 2010, the Cohasset School District in Massachusetts faced a public relations nightmare as a result of comments posted on Facebook by a science teacher. The 54 year-old teacher posted derogatory comments about her students and their parents. The science teacher assumed that the content on her Facebook page was accessible only by her friends, when in fact the settings were wide open. Shortly after several parents viewed her comments on Facebook, where she called her students "germ bags" and their parents "snobby" and "arrogant," the parents demanded her termination. It did not take long for the school district to demand her resignation, which she promptly provided. This issue, while resolved quickly, brought widespread international media attention to the matter, creating a significant distraction for the management and employees of the school district.

As these types of incidents occur with greater frequency, it has become very evident that the elimination of social media access does not in of itself effectively mitigate risk. In fact, some may argue that the risk to organizations is greater as a result of employees' social media activities that take place on their personal time versus while on the clock. Employee use of social media can be an extremely effective tool when properly used. However, a poorly managed employee-based social media effort can create nothing but headaches for an organization.

Social Media Challenges

As noted above, empowering employees with social media access in the workplace presents a number of organizational challenges. This section briefly describes the major challenges faced by organizations. The intent of this section is to ensure that organizations that enable employee social media usage are fully aware of the risks, and as such, are able to develop the means to mitigate the risks.

Loss of Productivity: Opponents of social media usage in the workplace claim that valuable organizational resources are wasted when employees are permitted to access social media platforms at work. Lost productivity comes in the form of the employee's paid time that is spent browsing social media platforms for personal reasons, rather than having the employee focused on the organization's business. Examples of such activity include employee use of social media-based games such as FarmVille, Mafia Wars, etc. Other examples include employee use of social media-based chat as well as the browsing of friend profiles. It is noted, however, that any type of Internet access granted to employees can result in lost productivity.

Liability Related to Employee Comments: Organizations may be accountable for inappropriate comments made by an employee on a social media platform. Inappropriate comments may affect other employees as well as third parties. Such comments may include derogatory, discriminatory or harassing language that results in some form of action against the organization. To the extent that the employee is deemed to be acting on behalf of the organization, there exists potential risk to the organization.

Inability to Discipline Employees: Organizations are challenged to some degree when disciplining employees for actions related to social media-based comments deemed inappropriate by the organization. The challenge relates to discipline against employees for derogatory comments made about the organization. Protections provided to employees by the National Labor Relations Act and the First Amendment (as well as other similar state statutes), prohibit employers from taking disciplinary action in certain cases. As such, in certain circumstances employers may be helpless against employees that post disparaging and damaging comments regarding the organization.

Disclosure of Confidential Information: Employees may intentionally or inadvertently disclose confidential information about the organization or its customers. Disclosure may take many forms. For example, an employee working on a confidential project may inadvertently "leak" information about the project on a social media status update prior to the formal unveiling of the product or service. This leak may affect the organization's public relations plan as well as may prematurely tip off the competition, reducing the effectiveness of a scheduled product/service launch. Another form of disclosure may include the release of internal operational "company secrets" that reveals to the competition how the company maintains its competitive advantage. Such disclosures may also affect customers to the extent that confidential customer information is disclosed. These actions may also have the effect of voiding proprietary intellectual property rights, waiving attorney/client protection as well as violating applicable federal and state securities and privacy laws.

<u>Organizational Versus Personal Social Media Usage</u>

To the extent that employees are permitted to use social media in the workplace, the organization must address the questions below in order to determine the process for managing the risk. The answers to these questions should be included in the organization's social media policy.

- Will any employees be permitted to access social media at work for personal use?

- Will any employees be permitted to access social media at work for business use?

- If some or all of the organization's employees are permitted to access social media for business use, will they be encouraged to use their personal accounts or will they be provided with company accounts?

Determining Access to Social Media for Personal Use: Once an organization decides to grant social media access to employees, it must determine if the access will be universal or if it will be provided only to certain "qualified" employees. Factors that should be considered in making this decision include (but are not limited to) the organization's general policy on providing internet access to employees, the availability of Internet-accessible equipment within the organization, the organization's overall social media strategy, the ability and intent of the organization to monitor social media usage to prevent abuse, and other relevant factors that may influence the organization's decision. The organization's management should evaluate this information prior to establishing its policy for employee use of social media in the workplace.

Determining Use of Social Media for Business Purpose: To the extent that employees are granted business-use social media access, the organization should determine how it will incorporate social media-enabled employees into the organization's business practices. For example, an organization may limit participation to a small percentage of employees. These employees would be officially tasked with creating outbound social media messages on behalf of the organization. The employees would be personally involved in responding to messaging, such as comments on review sites, social network sites, etc. Due to the inherent risks associated with employee use of social media, any employees provided with social media privileges should be required to complete a social media training program.

Personal Versus Organizational Accounts: Organizations that permit employees to use social media for business purposes must determine whether employees may utilize their personal accounts or whether they must use organization-controlled accounts.

While permitting employees to use their own accounts is quick and simple, organizations must contend with two major challenges: First, accounts that are owned by employees are difficult to monitor for compliance with the organization's social media and other applicable policies because the login credentials are held by the employee. Few employees would be willing to participate in a social media program if it required them to divulge the login credentials for their personal social media accounts. Further, requiring access to the employee-owned accounts may violate laws such as the federal Stored Communications Act, as well as the Fourth Amendment.

An additional concern is the comingling of employees' personal messages with the organization's messages. Depending on the content maintained on an employee's social media account, the organization may inadvertently place its reputation at risk by comingling messages. Rather than rely on using employee personal accounts for social media purposes, the organization should establish social media accounts that are owned and controlled by the organization. Once established, these accounts should be monitored for compliance with the social media policy.

One exception to the recommendation on not using personal accounts for business purposes is the use of personal accounts for infrequent ad hoc support of the organization. Occasionally an employee will come upon an opportunity to take part in a social media conversation that involves the organization. The employee's input may be in response to a posted question or a clarification of an issue. In such a case, the organization may benefit from a knowledgeable employee's input. In such cases, the organization may find it beneficial to permit employees to interact using a personal account. However, any employees provided such authority should be adequately trained to ensure compliance with the organization's social media policy.

Employees as Brand Ambassadors

Every employee should be treated as a "Brand Ambassador", regardless of an organization's social media strategy. Brand Ambassadors represent the organization to the outside world and attempt to positively influence that world to the benefit of the organization. "Brand Ambassador"s are what current and potential customers see when they interact with an employee. Prior to social media, "Brand Ambassador"s conducted most of their influencing outside of the Internet, through face-to-face social and business functions such as chamber of commerce, Rotary and other meetings. Today, social media has enabled "Brand Ambassador"s to use tools such as social networks, blogs, and other forms of social media, to conduct their influencing activities.

According to Tom Blackett in *Brands and Branding* (Bloomberg Press, 2009), "when employees are excited by the proposition they will help to sustain it and communicate it to customers, suppliers and others through their enthusiasm and commitment." Therefore, to the extent that an organization can properly motivate its employees to act as "Brand Ambassador"s, employees can become an incredibly effective tool for influencing stakeholders. As such, the maintenance of a strong cadre of "Brand Ambassador"'s will result in a stronger brand, improved customer satisfaction, increased revenue and strong financial results.

Organizations may choose to empower and unleash "Brand Ambassador"'s in the social media universe by granting them social media access in the workplace. Depending on the organization's social media strategy, these employees may use either personal or organizational social media accounts to represent the organization. However, before unleashing the "Brand Ambassador"'s, the employees must understand their role and recognize that their actions may have a direct effect on the organization, and ultimately, the organization's success.

"Brand Ambassador" success requires that employees commit to the organization's code of conduct (e.g., respectful tone, free of profanity, etc.) whenever they interact on a social media platform. Employees must understand that actions taken on social media platforms may not be differentiated as the actions made by an individual and as such, may be interpreted as organization-sanctioned activity. Therefore, whether on or off the clock, employees must be aware of the effect that their interactions on social media platforms can have on the organization.

Blogger Linda Tucci describes in the TotalCIO blog at TechTarget.com ("*Social Media Risks That Will Make Your Hair Stand on End*") an instance involving an executive at a public relations firm. The seasoned public relations executive was flying to meet with a major client. Upon arriving at the client's hometown, the public relations executive tweeted that the client's hometown was one of those places he would rather die than have to live in. An employee of the client's firm read the tweet and passed it on to senior officials at the client and the public relations firm. To say that the public relations executive had some explaining to do is an understatement. The embarrassment caused to the public relations firm by its executive was further exacerbated by the fact that the public relations executive was meeting with the client to pitch, of all things, social media communications!

The public relations executive story noted above is an example of a major concern with social media. As more and more employees use social media for personal reasons, more and more of the employees' personal conversations will unintentionally cross over into the employees' professional lives. Consider an employee that posts an inappropriate (from the organization's point of view) comment on a LinkedIn group. The comment could be directly attributed to the organization based on information contained on the employee's LinkedIn profile. Or consider an employee that posts an inappropriate photo on Flickr while in a company uniform. The point is that even if the organization restricts employee use of social media at work or even if the organization chooses to not to participate in social media altogether, there is still potential risk arising from the activities of employees while on their own time. These employee activities may create uncomfortable, damaging and even legal liability for the organization. Employees should understand that they are all "Brand Ambassadors" and that being a "Brand Ambassador" means acting and responding in an appropriate manner. Anything less may result in significant damage to the organization.

In an effort to minimize risk resulting from the personal social media use of employees, organizations may include in the social media policy a requirement that states that employees keep the organization's logo and other protected intellectual property off of the employees' personal social network pages, blogs, profiles, etc. The organization may also prohibit employees from using the organization's e-mail address when registering for personal-use social media sites. With respect to employees that maintain personal blogs, the organization should require that employees include a disclaimer that the views expressed on the blog are those of the employee and not of the organization.

Social media is built upon the concepts of honesty and transparency. The social media community is not very forgiving when it comes to companies and employees that share information that is intentionally misleading or altogether fraudulent. While inadvertently incorrect information can be forgiven, it is best to have employees comment honestly and with complete information or not at all. In addition to the issues of honesty and transparency is the issue of protocol. Paul Gillin, in his book *The New Influencers* (Quill Driver Books, 2009), states that the social media community "is developing into an extraordinarily civil and deferential culture." As such, rude and uncivilized behavior is also not tolerated and can reflect poorly on the organization.

While companies should encourage civility, honesty and transparency when interacting on social media platforms, certain information should be off-limits and not disclosed by employees. This information includes confidential company and customer information, information related to legal disputes and other sensitive information. The release of this type of information should be reserved for senior management.

Organizations should have an incident response process in place to deal with employee social media comments that create a need for action. Further, the social media policy should enable the organization to demand that employees remove any damaging comments. The policy should state that compliance with this requirement is a condition of employment. Further, employees should understand that noncompliance with the social media policy may result in disciplinary action, up to and including termination.

Employees are every organization's most trusted ally. Through social media, organizations are able to unleash them in a manner that transforms employees into advocates for the organization, evangelizing through their social networks on behalf of the organization. In the 1980's there was a Faberge Shampoo commercial that spoke of users of the shampoo telling two friends and those friends telling two friends, and so on and so on. Fast forward 20 years. Now imagine an organization's employees telling their friends, and their friends telling their friends and so on and so on. With proper policies and training, employees as "Brand Ambassador"'s can go a long way in maximizing the organization's brand with the help of social media.

While every organization would like to believe that its employees are smart, capable and masters of common sense, every employee has the potential to "blow it" every now and then. As such, every organization must address through a formal, written social media policy, employee use of social media – whether or not employees are communicating on social media in an "official" capacity.

The social media policy should provide guidance to employees regarding the topics that are open for discussion. Organizations operating in largely unregulated environments can provide simple guidance such as requesting that employees use common sense. Organizations that operate in tightly regulated industries (e.g., securities, banking, healthcare, etc.) should, at a minimum, provide topics that are off-limits due to regulatory restrictions. These topics can include legal matters (potential or current litigation), financial information (e.g., earnings results/expectations, etc.), and other topics specific to each regulated industry.

Let Employees Respond in their Own Voice

To the extent that an organization permits employees to act in an official capacity, the employees should be given the latitude to respond in their own voice as long as they are complying with the organization's social media policy and code of conduct.

For example, employees of a surf board maker interacting on social media platforms should be permitted to use their personal voice as well as jargon and mannerisms consistent with their industry. Likewise, employees of a bank catering to high net worth individuals should be permitted to respond in a manner consistent with the expectations for such an organization while keeping their individuality. Organizations should be cautious about putting too many restrictions on the tone of their employees' communications. A policy that places too many restrictions on employees will minimize the potential for community building on social media.

Placing too many restrictions may also turn out to be a legal concern. In Connecticut, the Teamsters' Union filed a complaint with the National Labor Relations Board regarding an employer's social media policy. According to the lawsuit, the social media policy violated the employees' rights by implementing a policy that was overly broad as to effectively preclude employees from engaging in the protected concerted activity of discussing workplace conditions and terms of employment. A second lawsuit originated when a teacher's union in Florida filed a similar lawsuit alleging that a *proposed* social media policy was overly broad so as to violate the right to free speech pursuant to the First Amendment.

According to the *IBM Social Computing Guidelines* (http://www.ibm.com/blogs/zz/en/guidelines.html), employees at IBM that interact on blogs, wikis, social networks, virtual worlds and social media, are instructed to "use your own voice; bring your own personality to the forefront." This message is consistent at many other organizations, large and small, that understand the benefit to unleashing their cadre of social media-enabled employees. These organizations recognize that employees will not act on behalf of the organization if they cannot do so in their own words. Therefore, an effective social media policy provides employees with sufficient flexibility to be heard in their own voice.

Honest and Transparent Communications

Social media is said to be successful primarily due to its communal characteristics that include sharing in an honest and transparent manner. The beauty of social media is that it is a self-regulating and self-correcting medium where the participants, or "community members," call out other community members whose social media activities have been found to be questionable – particularly those that are trying to use the system to their advantage. According to Paul Gillin in his book, *The New Influencers*, "millions of writers of all ages, interests, languages and motivations are together forming a set of shared principles, operating standards and behaviors without any kind of central coordination."

This phenomenon has created a system that places significant value on honest and straightforward communication over salesman-like puffery. Any time an employee undertakes social media activities with the intent to mislead, the employee places the organization at risk from both a reputational and legal perspective.

From the reputational risk perspective, the danger lies in the potential of a backlash by the social media community, resulting from the misleading statements made by an employee. Such a backlash can cause serious harm to an organization as a result of negative publicity.

Blogger Lisa Brauner describes the concept of honesty and transparency on the *Workplace Privacy Counsel* blog (http://privacyblog.littler.com). Her article entitled "*Caveat Employer: Let the Employer Beware of Employee Endorsements on Social Media Websites*," very clearly defines why honesty and transparency are not only a necessity from a public relations perspective, but also from a legal perspective.

According to Ms. Brauner, organizations must be aware of the risks posed as a result of product and service endorsements made by employees on social media platforms. Ms. Brauner notes that organizations are subject to the October 2009 Federal Trade Commission guidance (*Guides Concerning Use of Endorsements and Testimonials in Advertising*), which protects consumers from misleading endorsements and advertising. The Federal Trade Commission guidance makes clear that employers whose employees use social media to make misleading comments regarding their employer's products or services, face potential liability, even in cases where the employer has no knowledge of the employee's social media activities.

The Federal Trade Commission guidance states that employees endorsing their employer's products or services must disclose to their audience their relationship to an employer at the time they provide the endorsement or testimonial. If employees make misleading statements about the employer's products and services that result in injury to consumers, the Federal Trade Commission may bring an enforcement action against the employer. Ms. Brauner also states that postings on social media platforms can reach wide audiences and as such, employers may be vulnerable to large-scale liability such as class-action lawsuits by consumers and/or legal action by state attorney generals.

In August 2010, the Federal Trade Commission announced its first social media-based settlement. The defendant was a public relations company that represented a videogame company. According to the Federal Trade Commission's press release (*Public Relations Firm to Settle FTC Charges that It Advertised Clients' Gaming Apps Through Misleading Online Endorsements*), the public relations agency "engaged in deceptive advertising by having employees pose as ordinary consumers posting game reviews at the online iTunes store, and not disclosing that the reviews came from paid employees working on behalf of the developers." The press release further stated that "companies, including public relations firms involved in online marketing, need to abide by long-held principles of truth in advertising. Advertisers should not pass themselves off as ordinary consumers touting a product, and endorsers should make it clear when they have financial connections to sellers."

For publicly traded companies, honesty and transparency also has implications relative to Rule 10b-5. According to Investopedia.com, Rule 10b-5 is "a regulation formally known as the Employment of Manipulative and Deceptive Practices that was created under the Securities Exchange Act of 1934. This rule deems it to be illegal for anybody to directly or indirectly use any measure to defraud, make false statements, omit relevant information or otherwise conduct operations of business that would deceive another person; in relation to conducting transactions involving stock and other securities."

The need for transparency and honesty, however, does not mean that employees should disclose confidential company and customer information or proprietary information (e.g., trade secrets, etc.) that can have an adverse effect on the organization. Being honest and transparent does not mean that all information should be shared.

Based upon the public relations and legal risks posed by misleading comments on social media platforms, it is very clear that organizations should develop a formal, written social media policy that ensures that employee interactions are conducted in an honest manner and consistent with the norms of the social media community.

Employee Disclaimers

One of social media's greatest benefits is the ability of organizations to unleash its employees as "Brand Ambassador"s. Empowering employees in this manner allows organizations to leverage human capital with the purpose of creating dialogue with stakeholders on a more personal level. Each "Brand Ambassador" is able to take advantage of opportunities that arise in the social media universe that may enhance the organization's brand.

While the leveraging of employees provides significant benefit to organizations, it is important for the social media community to recognize when an employee's social media interactions are personal activities that do not belong to the organization. Personal messages may not be aligned with the company's mission or vision and as such, may create confusion to the extent that the messages are perceived to be "official" organizational messages. The use of a simple disclaimer at the appropriate time by employees informs the social media community that the activities are personal and not an official communication. The disclaimer may protect the organization against improper, inaccurate or incorrect statements while preserving the employee's ability to express an opinion.

An example is a company-supported blog where employees are permitted to express their opinions. While these blogs may be stored on company servers, the employees may not be required to "toe the company line." While in all cases the employees' interactions should be consistent with the company's rules on confidentiality and conduct, the employees' blog posts may at times appear to contradict organizational policies or practices.

In order to eliminate criticism by the social media community and other stakeholders, the organization should require all employees to accompany personal social media comments and other activities with a disclaimer, to the extent that such activity can be misconstrued as an organization-sanctioned activity. This includes, but is not limited to, employee blogs, online articles, and other activities where the employee's affiliation with the organization is known or can be easily determined. Including this requirement within the organization's formal, written social media policy will assist the organization in mitigating a significant amount of risk associated with employee personal social media activity.

Protecting Intellectual Property Rights

One of the Golden Rules of social media is "give credit where credit due." Social media not only provides an avenue for self-expression, it also provides the ability to easily share digital work, whether a blog post, pdf file, video file, audio file, or some other form of digital work. Employees that post information on social media platforms should be trained to always give credit where credit is due – particularly if the work is protected by copyright. In addition, when employees are acting as "Brand Ambassador"s, employees must be careful not to post anything that they have no permission to post. This includes videos, music, photos, written works and anything else that has the ability to be shared online.

With any rule there are always exceptions. For example, a newspaper, blog or other Internet-based site may explicitly provide a "sharing" option that allows the user to cross-post the copyrighted material. In such instances, although the work is protected by copyright, the "sharing" option provides the user with permission to post the information elsewhere.

Another sharing option is sharing through use of the Fair Use rule. The following excerpt of the Fair Use rule is taken from the Web site of the National Council of Teachers of English (www.ncte.org).

"Law provides copyright protection to creative works in order to foster the creation of culture. Its best known feature is protection of owners' rights. But copying, quoting, and generally re-using existing cultural material can be, under some circumstances, a critically important part of generating new culture. In fact, the cultural value of copying is so well established that it is written into the social bargain at the heart of copyright law. The bargain is this: we as a society give limited property rights to creators to encourage them to produce culture; at the same time, we give other creators the chance to use that same copyrighted material, without permission or payment, in some circumstances. Without the second half of the bargain, we could all lose important new cultural work."

While employees need to be aware not to violate the rights of copyright holders, many copyright owners explicitly permit sharing by way of sharing buttons. In other cases, the nature and manner in which copyrighted works are shared may be covered under the Fair Use rule.

In an effort to simplify and ensure compliance, the organization's formal, written social media policy should require employees to utilize "share" buttons or share URL links to the copyright owner's site – rather than upload or paste a copy of the work. This will protect both the employee and the organization from potential litigation from a copyright owner.

Expectation of Privacy

Marc Gobé, in his book *Emotional Branding*, says "the Web is a place where, in the greatest of paradoxes, freedom means that the whole world knows what you are doing in certain cases almost minute by minute. By voluntarily breaking the last walls of our privacy, our lives become an open canvas for our best friends or the people we trust."

Social media by name and design is a "social" media. It is not called "private media" for a very specific reason – there is nothing private about it. Regardless of privacy settings and other controls, increasingly courts around the country are sending the following message to American workers: "employees using social media should not be under the false impression of a right and expectation of privacy in the workplace." These court cases are concluding that personal social media use in the workplace is not protected and as such, information contained within social media platforms may be subject to discovery during the legal process as well as part of other procedures such as audits, background checks and similar activities that benefit from the use of information contained on social networks.

In today's open and social media-enabled society, we live our lives more openly and transparently than ever before, sharing everything from our choice of breakfast cereal in the morning to photos of our children to our location in real-time. For the most part, there are fewer and fewer secrets being kept as more and more of us become increasingly comfortable giving up more of our information than ever before. While the evidence does not suggest that every life should be an open book, recent judicial decisions appear to take a practical approach when it comes to information contained on social media platforms. In a sense, employees are not going to be allowed to act to the detriment of an organization and then hide behind a form of social media immunity.

From the organization's point of view, the assumption of the lack of privacy plays a key role in managing employees' use of social media within the workplace. Based upon the current direction of case law, it is in every organization's best interest to disclose the organization's right to inspect social media-based records to the extent such records originated through the use of the organization's assets, including computers, network infrastructure and company-controlled/owned social media accounts. The disclosure should be clear about its right to monitor social media interactions in real-time (network monitoring), in stored files (caches, temporary files, etc), while on "company time" and using the organization's equipment. Such a policy statement will assist the organization in defeating opposition to demands for information during the legal process, should it be required, and will provide protection against claims of invasion of privacy.

In *City of Ontario v. Quon*, a California police officer had his case ultimately reach the United States Supreme Court when the police officer was verbally told by a supervisor that he indeed did have an expectation of privacy when using for personal use a department-issued digital device – a statement that contradicted the employer's written policy. While a lower court supported Officer Quon's assertion that his personal electronic messages were protected based upon the verbal assurance, the U.S. Supreme Court eventually determined that the officer did not have an expectation of privacy on the basis that: 1) a formal written policy existed; 2) the device used was provided by the employer, and as such, the employer had the right to monitor appropriate usage of its assets; and, 3) there was no less invasive and practical manner of monitoring general activity on the device.

In *Romano v. Steelcase, Inc.*, a New York trial concluded that an employee had no reasonable expectation of privacy regarding information posted on social networks – despite the restricted privacy settings established by the user. This case involved a plaintiff (employee) that was suing the employer over alleged permanent physical injuries incurred on the job. The employee attempted to keep out of court information that was contained on the employee's Facebook and MySpace pages. The employer sought this information to show a direct contradiction to the employee's claims regarding permanent injuries. The court sided with the employer.

While recent legal decisions appear to support the organizational assertion against an expectation of privacy in the workplace, organizations must still tread carefully to prevent violations of the Stored Communications Act. The Stored Communications Act prohibits employers from, among other things, accessing employee accounts maintained by third-party hosts such as social networks. The Stored Communications Act generally allows organizations to access stored communications such as emails and other information stored within its own computer network. The Stored Communications Act, however, limits an organization's ability to access such information (without the employee's authorization) if it is stored by a third party service provider. A further complication is that even in instances where an employee has granted an employer access to third-party sites, such access may be deemed to be done under duress and as such, a violation of the Stored Communications Act. As such, experts generally recommend that employers not extend their reach beyond information contained within their systems in order to prevent violations of the Stored Communications Act.

In drafting the organization's social media policy, organizations should consult with their legal departments in order to determine how to best describe an organization's policy regarding the expectation of privacy and the monitoring of social media activities. Further, each organization should work with its legal department to determine the applicable local, state and federal laws. Once the policy is implemented, organizations should avoid any deviation which may result in questioning whether or not the employee had an expectation of privacy due to "practices" that are inconsistent with the written policy.

Employee Training

As the phrase goes, "if a tree falls in the woods and no one hears it, does it make any noise?" Similarly, if an organization crafts a social media policy but does not provide training to its employees on the contents of the policy, does it do any good? Creating the social media policy is only part of the solution to mitigating the risks associated with social media in the workplace.

In order to ensure that the social media policy achieves the expected results the organization must establish a social media training program that includes the following elements:

- <u>Training Needs Assessment</u> – Organizations conduct training needs assessments to ensure that employees have the knowledge and tools necessary to do their jobs. The training needs assessment determines the type of social media training required by each employee to ensure that the organization receives the maximum benefit from the social media policy and its social media strategy. It is important to note that not all employees require the same type of training. Most employees require only cursory training that touches upon the basics such as confidentiality, honesty, appropriate conduct, etc. Other employees, however, will require more extensive social media training. These employees include those that have been specifically selected to play a more involved role within the organization's social media strategy. Essentially, the type of training should be commensurate with the role that each employee will play. This training needs assessment determines the form of training (face-to-face, computer-based, etc.) as well as the depth of the training.

- <u>Measurable Outcomes</u> – Organizations should not only provide training – they should expect certain results from the money, time and effort spent in training employees. Organizations should create metrics (e.g., testing) by which to measure the success of its social media training program. While no specific metric will guarantee that employees will follow the policy, metrics such as multiple choice test will convey the importance of the policy to employees, resulting in greater diligence when performing applicable activities. Overall, the goal of social media training is success relative to compliance with the social media policy and the organization's social media-related strategic goals.

- Resources – To the extent possible, the social media training should be created by training professionals with a thorough knowledge of social media and the organization's social media policy and strategic plan. Based upon the size and complexity of the organization, the training resources may be limited. In such a case, it may be a good idea to have the training created and delivered (to the extent training is delivered face-to-face) by someone involved in the creation of the social media policy and/or strategic plan.

- Training Results – The social media policy and strategic plan are living breathing documents. As such, social media training is an evolutionary process. Since social media training is fairly new it will likely fall on one of the two extremes – too much training or too little training. Eventually, with time, feedback and practice, the training will be refined and improved. In order to make the social media training investment as worthwhile as possible, it is important to monitor the results of the training. Since each organization's social media strategy is unique, so is each social media policy. As such, each organization can create its own metrics to measure social media training success. At a minimum, organizations should follow-up with training participants once they have returned to their jobs to determine if the training was well received and appropriate relative to their job function.

Social Media-Based Terminations

As more and more employees lose their jobs for reasons related to social media, more and more social media-related lawsuits fill dockets across America's courts. Individual, class and union actions have employment law and technology experts paying close attention to these cases to determine the future landscape of social media within the workplace.

According to survey results contained in Proofpoint, Inc.'s (ProofPoint.com) report, *"Outbound Email and Data Loss Prevention in Today's Enterprise, 2010,"* the number of firms that reported social media-related terminations in 2010 remained consistent at seven percent compared to eight percent reported in the 2009 survey. However, this figure is nearly double the rate of four percent cited in the 2008 survey. This data suggests that there is definitely a need for organizations to consider the impact that social media will play in disciplining employees. The challenge for organizations is establishing the appropriate environment in which an organization can justifiably terminate an employee with the confidence of knowing that it will not likely experience a legal backlash.

According to attorney John R. Lanham, in the January 2010 edition of Morrison Foerster's (mofo.com) *Employment Law Commentary*, "employees' online communications may gain legal protection based on either the privacy or the substance of the communications." Mr. Lanham's article brought to light two very real risks for organizations: 1) the growth of social media-related lawsuits; and, 2) current and developing legislation intended to protect employees from employment-related actions on the basis of things said on social media platforms.

In *Pietrylo, et al. v. Hillstone Restaurant Group d/b/a Houston's*, two employees of a Hackensack, New Jersey Houston's Restaurant successfully sued their former employer in an unlawful termination case that stemmed from the employees' use of social media to disparage the restaurant and its management. In this case, the two employees were terminated for establishing an invitation-only MySpace page for the purpose of allowing employees to vent their dissatisfaction with their employer. Those invited to join the group were existing and former employees – none of which included management.

Management eventually became aware of the MySpace page through an employee that belonged to the MySpace group. The employee provided management with the login ID and password to access the invitation-only MySpace page. In response to the derogatory information posted on the MySpace page about Houston's management and the company, the two employees that created the MySpace page were terminated for violating the restaurant's "core values." The two employees sued Houston's in federal court and received a favorable ruling in June 2009 when the court found that management had violated the federal Stored Communications Act, as well as a comparable state law. The violations were based on the manner in which management gained access to the site. According to the court, the employee that provided management with the user ID and password was perceived to be under duress and feared retaliatory action by management if the user ID and password were not provided.

In another case in October 2010, the National Labor Relations Board filed a complaint in Connecticut against American Medical Response of Connecticut, Inc ("AMRC"). The complaint alleges that AMRC violated the National Labor Relations Act when it terminated an employee for making disparaging comments on her Facebook page regarding a supervisor. The National Labor Relations Board alleges that AMRC's social media policy, which prohibits employees from depicting adversely AMRC in any way on Facebook or other social media sites where pictures of the employees can be posted, violates the National Labor Relations Act.

The National Labor Relations Act prohibits employers from punishing workers – whether or not they are union members – for discussing working conditions or unionization. The National Labor Relations Board claims that this is a case of employees utilizing a social media platform for the purpose of discussing jointly matters related to working conditions, a permissible activity under the National Labor Relations Act. The National Labor Relations Board alleges that AMRC's social media policy was overly broad and denied employees' the right to discuss working conditions among themselves.

These two examples illustrate the human resources-related challenges that employers currently face when dealing with social media in the workplace. In an effort to keep employees from publicly discussing on social media platforms personal employment-related issues, employees should be encouraged to bring forward complaints to the Human Resources Department or a company ombudsman.

Another issue related to employee terminations and social media is the topic of reference letters. Reference letters come into play after an employee has been terminated. In most cases reference letters are requested by former employees when the termination was for a reason other than "for cause" such as a reduction in force ("RIF") or a similar event. At other times, however, employees terminated "for cause" may seek reference letters from managers and employees not involved in the decision to terminate or with whom the terminated employee has a close professional or personal relationship. While many organizations look favorably upon reference letters for terminated employees, some organizations do not provide them. Many organizations will provide, upon request, generic reference letters that speak primarily to the tenure, position and other objective facts related to employment rather than address qualitative aspects of the former employee.

Based upon the popularity of profession-based social media platforms such as LinkedIn, it is important for organizations to address instances in which such reference letters are permitted. In today's environment, it is very likely that a terminated employee will seek an online reference from a past manager or co-worker in an effort to assist the former employee in securing new employment. In developing a policy statement regarding reference letters, it is important for the organization to convey to employees through its policy and training that online recommendations such as those provided through LinkedIn, are equivalent to reference letters and as such, employees must comply with the organization's policy regarding reference letters.

Employment law is an extremely complex and evolving area of law. As such, this book cannot adequately address all of the issues related to social media and unemployment law. This guidance is intended to assist organizations in developing an effective social media policy that addresses key employment-related concerns. Unfortunately, employment law relative to social media usage is currently taking shape. As such, it is somewhat difficult to fully define best practices. Regardless, a well thought out approach that incorporates common sense business practices and evolving case law will provide the best protection.

Action Items

Recruitment Through Social Media

☐ Determine whether the organization will permit the use of information taken from social media sites as part of the information used in evaluating job candidates. The social media policy should clearly note the organization's position regarding the use of such information in the recruitment process. In lieu of a statement in the social media policy regarding the use of social media in the recruiting process, the organization may consider including this information in the organization's human resources policy. Regardless of the location of the policy statement regarding the use of social media in the recruiting process, the organization should provide training to all personnel responsible for evaluating job candidates in order to ensure compliance with the policy as well as any other applicable laws, rules and regulations.

☐ If the organization permits the use of information gathered from social media sites as part of the job candidate evaluation process, the policy should state the type of information that may be gathered, documented, and considered. This section of the policy requires the assistance of human resources personnel familiar with laws, rules and regulations related to permissible and prohibited information relative to employment applications, applicable "legal activities" laws, and applicable sections of the National Labor Relations Act and Fair Credit Reporting Act.

☐ When possible, personnel responsible for gathering social media-based information relative to job applications, should not be involved in the candidate evaluation process to avoid potential criticism regarding the consideration of prohibited information that may have been observed during the social media background investigation.

☐ If the organization will consider the use of social media-based information as part of the applicant evaluation process, the organization should include a disclosure in its application package that states that publicly available information, including information contained on social media sites, may be considered in the applicant evaluation.

Employee Use of Social Media

☐ Determine whether the organization will permit employees to access social media platforms during the work day. If so, the organization should determine which employees will be granted such access. Further, the organization should determine if access will permit personal use, business use, or both. The organization should also determine if employees will use personal accounts for business-purpose use or if they will use organization-issued (recommended) social media accounts. If organization-controlled accounts are issued, the establishment and maintenance of the accounts should be centralized (e.g., Information Technology Department).

☐ The organization should provide social media "Brand Ambassador" training to all employees to inform employees of the pros and cons related to the use of social media. This training should address all applicable sections of the organization's social media policy, including code of conduct, information security, harassment, and any applicable regulatory requirements (e.g., NASD, SEC, FTC, etc.).

☐ The organization should provide a copy of the social media policy to each employee and require the employee to sign an acknowledgment that evidences receipt and understanding of the policy. This process alerts the employee to the serious nature of the social media policy and will encourage the employee to comply with the social media policy.

☐ The organization should develop and implement a social media incident response plan. In lieu of an incident response plan in the social media policy, the organization may consider including "social media" events as part of the organization's overall incident response plan. Regardless of the location of the policy statement regarding incident response to social media events, the organization should provide applicable training to all personnel in order to ensure that employees report to the appropriate personnel any social media activity that requires an organizational response.

☐ The organization should provide all employees with its policy statement regarding the organization's right to monitor employee activity, including social media activity (comments, photos, videos, etc), and the lack of an expectation of privacy. In lieu of a lack of expectation of privacy policy, the organization may consider including "social media" activities as part of the organization's overall employee monitoring policy that covers other activities such as e-mail, Web sites, etc. In such as case, the revised policy should be provided to all employees.

☐ The organization should forbid employees from requesting job applicants to "friend," "like" or otherwise permit an employee to gain access to any information that is not "publicly available." This requirement will assist the organization in complying with the federal Stored Communications Act and similar state statutes.

☐ The organization should conduct a social media training needs assessment to determine the type of training that is needed for the organization's employees. Training should be conducted and updated as deemed necessary, but at least on an annual basis.

<u>Social Media-Based Terminations</u>

☐ The organization should determine its reference letter policy for terminated and other former employees. In lieu of a statement in the social media policy regarding the use of reference letters, the organization may consider including this information in the organization's human resources policy. Regardless of the location of the policy statement regarding reference letters, the organization should make all personnel aware of the policy in order to ensure compliance with the policy.

☐ The organization should establish a program that permits employees to file confidential complaints with the Human Resources Department or a company ombudsman to prevent employees from complaining about the company on social media platforms.

CONCLUSION

As stated at the beginning of this Guide, the intent is to make the case that all organizations, regardless of their involvement in social media activities, are subject to social media risks in the workplace. These risks must be properly managed in order to prevent costly harm to an organization's reputation and profitability. The previous chapter provided a description of the potential risks. It also provided a list of action items that organizations should implement to protect against those risks.

As shown in this Guide, social media use is ubiquitous. Social media activity is rapidly blurring the line between personal and business use. As more and more employees join the social media revolution, the risks to organizations significantly increase. It is no longer acceptable to ignore social media and expect the organization to be insulated from social media risks. Today, regardless of organizational social media strategy – or lack of social media strategy, an organization must implement policies and procedures that address the risks brought in by employees.

Some readers of this Guide may opine that the intent of this Guide is to discourage social media usage. That is far from the truth. Social media can bring significant value to any organization if it is managed properly. From increased brand awareness to increased sales, social media has the potential to dramatically improve any organization's financial results. As such, the goal of this Guide is to allow organizations to make a complete and honest assessment of their individual situation and to tackle these risks with their eyes wide open. Many organizations have held off on implementing a social media strategy based on their lack of knowledge regarding the risks. This Guide assists those organizations by providing a tool that identifies the risks that exist from a human resources perspective, in order to give management the knowledge to make sound decisions. Other organizations have implemented social media strategies without fully understanding the risks. This Guide will provide those managers with a tool that will allow them to sleep better.

This Guide was written at the start of 2011. With social media evolving so quickly it is possible that the types of sites may increase, the names of the popular social media sites may change, and the number participants will continue to grow. New risks may also emerge along the way. Since risks that manifest themselves tend to have an adverse affect on an organization's reputation and profitability, an organization that addresses the risks identified in this Guide will develop a competitive advantage in its industry. Further, as new risks evolve, the organization will be better prepared to identify and manage the new risks.

In the spirit of social media, readers are encouraged to join the conversation by joining the community at SocialMediaRiskManagement.com. Also, any comments for improvement to this Guide can be emailed to HRGuide@SocialMediaRiskManagement.com.

ABOUT THE AUTHOR

Jesse Torres is a banker and social media enthusiast. Jesse has spent nearly 20 years in leadership and executive management positions in risk management, internal audit, regulatory compliance, operations, information technology and marketing. Jesse began his career as a bank examiner with the Office of the Comptroller of the Currency ("OCC") and then as a Senior Consultant for KPMG Peat Marwick's financial services practice. Recently, Jesse has held executive management positions in several financial institutions ranging from $250 million in asset size to over $6 billion.

Jesse has authored several e-books, including the *Community Bankers Guide to Social Network Marketing*, the *Community Bankers Guide to Hispanic Marketing*, and *Creating an Ironclad Social Media Policy*.

Jesse is a frequent conference speaker and is often interviewed by the media regarding social media. He holds a B.A. from UCLA and is a graduate of the Pacific Coast Banking School. He regularly writes columns for industry periodicals and teaches community college marketing courses.

Jesse can be reached by email at MrJesseTorres@gmail.com or on Twitter @JSTORRES.

BIBLIOGRAPHY

Allen, Brad, "IROs Adapt Social Media to Extend Reach," *Inside Investor Relations*, November 2, 2010, *http://www.insideinvestorrelations.com/ articles/16618/iros-adapt-social-media-extend-reach.*

Aquila, Frank, "Investor Relations in the Age of Social Media," *Practicing Law Institute Securities Law Practice Center*, November 23, 2010, *http://seclawcenter.pli.edu/ 2010/11/23/investor-relations-in-the-age-of-social-media/.*

Bennett, Christopher P., Amy J. Greer, Jacob Thride, "Social Media in Action in the Securities Sector," *Legal Bytes*, March 8, 2010, *http://www.legalbytes.com /tags/regulation-fd.*

Blanchette, Sharon and Pam Buckley, "Financial Institutions and Social Media: The 'Upside' and Traditional View of Risk," *California Banker Magazine*, July/August 2010, *pgs. 8-9, 30.*

Bodine, Larry, "Employees Have No Expectation of Privacy in Facebook or MySpace Profiles," *Larry Bodine Law Marketing Blog*, October 26,

2010, *http://blog. larrybodine.com/2010/10/articles/tech/employees-have-no-expectation-of-privacy-in-facebook-or-myspace-profiles/.*

Boris, Cynthia, "Courts Disagree on Expectation of Privacy Regarding Social Media, "*Marketing Pilgrim,* September 30, 2010, *http://www.marketingpilgrim.com/2010/09/courts-disagree-on-expectation-of-privacy-regarding-social-media.html.*

DiBianca, Molly, "Teachers' Union Sues Over Proposed Social-Media Policy," *Delaware Employment Law Blog,* November 18, 2010, *http://www.delawareemploymentlawblog.com/2010/11/teachers_union_sues_over_propo.html.*

DiBianca, Molly, "5 Non-Negotiable Provisions for Your Social-Media Policy," *Delaware Employment Law Blog,* February 4, 2010, http://www.delawareemploymentlawblog.com/2010/02/5_nonnegotiable_provisions_for.html.

Dinan, Stephen, "Obama's Twitter Site Hacked?," *The Washington Times,* January 5, 2009, *http://www.washingtontimes.com/news/2009/jan/05/obamas-twitter-site-hacked.*

Drury, Glen. "Opinion Piece: Social Media: Should Marketers Engage and How Can It Be Done Effectively?" *Journal of Direct, Data and Digital Marketing Practice,* 2008. Vol. 9 No. 3 pp 274–277, *http://www. palgrave-journals.com/dddmp/journal/v9/n3/pdf/4350096a.pdf.*

Dykes, Trenton C., "Do Your Corporate Policies Consider Social Media?," *DLA News & Insights: Publications,* June 2, 2009, *http://www.dlapiper.com/do-your-corporate-policies-consider-social-media/.*

Ellis, Kathleen, "The Growing Risks of Social Media," *InsuranceJournal.com,* July 12, 2010, *http://www.insurancejournal.com/news/national/2010/07/12/111494.htm.*

Eggebrecht, Michael, "Top 8 Social Media Security Threats," *Information Security Resources,* August 17, 2009, *http://information-security-resources.com/2009/08/17/top-8-social-media-security-threats.*

Freed, Anthony, "Enterprise Information Security and Social Networks," *Infosec Island,* October 25, 2010, https://www.infosecisland.com/blogview/9137-Enterprise-Information-Security-and-Social-Networks.html.

Fridfinnson, Loa, "Advice: Monitoring Social Media," *Inside Investor Relations*, November 23, 2010, *http://www.insideinvestorrelations.com/ articles/16670/advice-monitoring-social-media.*

Fulkerson, Linda, "23 Types of Social Media Sites," *On Blogging Well*, February 17, 2010, *http://onbloggingwell.com/23-types-of-social-media-sites/.*

Gaudin, Sharon, "Group Lists Top Five Social Media Risks for Businesses," *Network World*, June 8, 2010, *http://www.networkworld. com/news/2010/060810-group-lists-top-five-social.html?page=1.*

Gesinsky, Loren, "Employer Social Media Policies: The Dangers of Too Much or Not Enough," *Gibbons P.C. Employment Law Alert*, November 12, 2010, http://www.employmentlawalert.com/2010/11/articles/ policieshandbooks/employer-social-media-policies-the-dangers-of-too-much-or-not-enough/

Goodchild, Joan, "Social Media Risks: The Basics," *CSO Online*, February 3, 2010, *http://www.csoonline.com/article/529764/social-media-risks-the-basics.*

Guerin, Lisa, "Facebook, MySpace, and Twitter (Oh, My)," *Nolo*, January 19, 2010, *http://www.employmentlegalblawg.com/2010/01/facebook-myspace-and-twitter-o.html.*

Henderson, Tom, "'Snobby' Parents Don't Care for Teacher's Facebook Post, Have Her Deleted," *ParentDish.com*, August 20, 2010, *http://www. parentdish.com/2010/08/20/snobby-parents-dont-care-for-teachers-face book-post-have-he/.*

Human, Tim, "IROs Remain Cagey About Social Media," *Inside Investor Relations*, November 18, 2010, *http://www.insideinvestorrelations.com /articles/16662/iros-remain-cagey-about-social-media.*

Jackson, Renee M., "Social Media Permeate the Employment Life Cycle," *The National Law Journal*, January 11, 2010, *http://www.law.com /jsp/nlj/PubArticleNLJ.jsp?id=1202437746082&slreturn=1&hbxlogin= 1.*

Jain, Sorav, "Fascinating Social Media Facts of Year 2010," *Social Media Today*, November 16, 2010, *http://socialmediatoday.com/soravjain/ 237864/fascinating-social-media-facts-year-2010.*

Jones, Dominic, "Why Regulation FD Shouldn't Keep You From Seeking Alpha," *IR Web Reporting International Inc.*, December 8, 2009, *http://irwebreport.com/20091208/ regulation-fd-eeking-alpha/*.

Keane, Brooke, "Social Networking Does Not Grant 'Expectation of Privacy,'" *PointParkGlobe.com*, October 28, 2009, *http://www. pointparkglobe.com/2.7416/social-networking-does-not-grant-expectation-of-privacy-1. 1039897*

Kim, Susanna, "NLRB Backs Worker Fired After Facebook Posts Ripping Boss" *abc NEWS*, November 10, 2010, *http://abcnews.go.com/Business/ facebook-firing-labor-board-takes-stand/story?id=12099395*

Lanham, John R., "Social Media in the Workplace," *Morrison Foerster Employment Law Commentary*, January 2010, Vol. 22, No. 1.

Lauby, Sharlyn, "Should You Search Social Media Sites for Job Candidate Information?," *American Express OPEN Forum*, August 31, 2010, http://www.openforum.com/idea-hub/topics/technology/article/should-you-search-social-media-sites-for-job-candidate-information-sharlyn-lauby

Marrow, Joseph C., "Securities Regulation and the Use of Social Media by Public Companies," Morse Barnes-Brown Pendleton PC, September 2009, *http://www.mbbp.com/ resources/business/social-media.html*.

McCrea, Bridget, "Managing Social Media Risks," *The Journal*, October 8, 2009, *http://thejournal.com/articles/2009/10/08/managing-social-media-risks.aspx?sc_lang=en*.

Ostrow, Adam, "Social Networking More Popular Than Email," *Mashable.com*, March 9, 2009, *http://mashable.com/2009/03/09/social-networking-more-popular-than-email/*.

Parekh, Neetal, "Fired for Facebook Use: Numbers Are Up," *Law & Daily Life*, August 13, 2009, http://blogs.findlaw.com/law_and_life/2009/08/fired-for-facebook-use-numbers-are-up.html

Reno, John, "Social Media Information Security – Pay Attention to Social Networks," *Red Spin Security Blog*, May 14, 2010, *http://www.redspin.com/blog/2010/05/14/social-meida-information-security-pay-attention-to-social-networks*.

Schmidt, Michael, "Social Media Advisor – Playing Nostradamus With Employment Law," *E-Discovery Law Review*, August 24, 2010, http://www.ediscoverylawreview. com/2010/08/articles/opinions/social-media-advisor-playing-nostradamus-with-employment-law/

Schnell, Garry J., "Online Social Media and SEC Regulations," *Davis Wright Tremaine LLP Corporate Finance Blog*, May 21, 2009, http://www.corpfinblog.com/2009/05/articles/federal-securities/online-social-media-and-sec-regulations.

Solis, Brian, "The Essential Guide to Social Media," *PR 2.0*, *http://BrianSolis.com*.

Stevens, Michael, "SMBs Embrace Social Media and Pay the Price," *Security Week*, September 15, 2010, *http://www.securityweek.com/smbs-embrace-social-media-and-pay-price*.

Sweeney, Ric, "'Brand Ambassadors' Give Your Business a Boost," *Business Courier*, April 15, 2002, http://www.bizjournals.com/cincinnati/stories/2002/04/15/smallb3.html.

Tucci, Linda, "Social Media Risks That Will Make Your Hair Stand on End," *TotalCIO.com*, August 20, 2010, http://itknowledgeexchange.techtarget.com/total-cio/social-media-risks-that-will-make-your-hair-stand-on-end/.

.

.com.   8

A

Amazon   8
Ambassador   24
American Medical Response of
    Connecticut, Inc   43
Answers.com   5

B

Barnes, Nora Ganim   10
Blackett, Tom   25
Blog Networks   7
Blogger   4
Blogging Communities   7
BlogHer.com   7
Blubrry.com   7
Brand Ambassador14, 24, 25, 27, 28,
    33, 34, 46
Brands and Branding   25
Brauner, Lisa   31

C

Caveat Employer
    Let the Employer Beware of
        Employee Endorsements on
        Social Media Websites   31
City of Ontario v. Quon   37
Classmates.com   6
Cohasset School District   20
Comment Communities   7
Content-Driven Communities   8

D

delicious.com   5
Deloitte LLP   1
    2009 Ethics &Workplace Survey   1
Digg   5
Disqus.   7

Drury, Glen   11

E

Ebay   8
eMarketer   13
Emotional Branding   36
employee recruitment   15
Employment Law Commentary   42
Employment of Manipulative and
    Deceptive Practices   32
evangelist   14
Examiner.com   7
expectation of privacy   39

F

Faberge Shampoo   28
Facebook   3, 5, 20, 38, 43
Fair Credit Reporting Act   17, 18, 46
Fair Use rule   35
FarmVille   21
Federal Trade Commission   31, 32
First Amendment   21, 30
Flickr   6, 26
Fourth Amendment   24
Fulkerson, Linda   4

G

Gawker.com   7
Gizmodo.com   7
Gobé, Marc   1, 36
Golden Age of Social Media   1
Google   6
Google Buzz   7
Guides Concerning Use of
    Endorsements and Testimonials
    in Advertising   31

I

IBM Social Computing Guidelines 30
IEBlog   4
Inc. 500   10
Investopedia.com   32

iTunes store   32

J

Jain, Sorav   4
Jezebel.com   7

L

Lanham, John R.   42
legal activities laws   16
LinkedIn   6, 26, 44
LiveJournal.com   7

M

Mafia Wars   21
Match.com   6
Mattson, Eric   10
Microblogging Sites   5
Microsoft   4
Middleton, Daina   9
MySpace   5, 38, 42

N

National Council of Teachers of
   English   35
National Labor Relations Act   17, 18,
   21, 43, 45
National Labor Relations Board   29,
   43
Niche Communities   6

O

On Blogging Well   4
Ostrow, Adam   4
Outbound Email and Data Loss
   Prevention in Today's Enterprise,
   2010   41

P

Paul Gillin   27, 30
Performics   9
Photo Sharing Sites   6

Pietrylo, et al. v. Hillstone Restaurant
   Group d/b/a Houston's   42
Podcasting Communities   7
Practical Law: The Journal   17
Presentation-Sharing Sites   7
Product-Based Communities   8
Professional Network Sites   6
Proofpoint, Inc.   41
Public Relations Firm to Settle FTC
   Charges that It Advertised
   Clients' Gaming Apps Through
   Misleading Online Endorsements
                                            32
publicly available information   17

R

reduction in force   44
Regional Social Media Sites   7
Romano v. Steelcase, Inc.   37
Rotary   25
Rule 10b-5   32

S

Securities Exchange Act of 1934   32
Shelfari.com   8
SlideShare.com   8
S-Net (The Impact of Social Media) 9
Social Bookmarking Sites   5
Social Email   7
social marketing   3
Social Measuring Sites   5
Social Media Adoption By U.S. Small
   Businesses Doubles Since 2009 11
Social Media in the Inc. 500: The
   First Longitudinal Study   10
Social Media in the Marketing Mix:
   Budgeting for 2011   13
Social Media Risks That Will Make
   Your Hair Stand on End   26
social media-based employment
   information   15
Social Networking Sites   5
Social News Sites   5
Social Q&A Sites   5
Social Search Sites   6
Solis, Brian   11

Stored Communications Act   24, 38, 42, 47

T

Teamsters' Union   29
Technorati   5
TechTarget.com   26
The Essential Guide to Social Media
                                                    11
The New Influencers   27, 30
Today at Vons   4
training needs assessment   39
TripAdvisor.com   8
Tucci , Linda   26
Twitpic   6
Twitter   5
TypePad   4

U

United States Supreme Court   37
University of Maryland's Smith
    School of Business   10

University of Massachusetts
    Dartmouth Center for Marketing
    Research   10
user-generated content   3

V

Video Sharing Sites   6
Vons   4

W

wiki   8
Wikipedia.org   8
WordPress   4
Workplace Privacy Counsel blog   31

Y

Yahoo   6
Yahoo! Answers   5
YouTube   6

www.ingramcontent.com/pod-product-compliance
Lightning Source LLC
Chambersburg PA
CBHW061032050326
40689CB00012B/2775